Contents

What are dolphins? 4

What is a dolphin school like? 6

Where do dolphins live? 8

How do dolphins swim? 10

What do dolphins eat? 12

How do dolphins find food? 13

How do dolphin schools hunt? 15

How do dolphins care for their young? 18

How do dolphins play and rest? 22

How do dolphins communicate? 24

Do dolphins fight? 26

What dangers do dolphin schools face? 27

Dolphin facts 29

Glossary 30

Find out more 31

Index 32

Any words appearing in the text in bold, **like this**, are explained in the Glossary.

What are dolphins?

Some of the world's dolphins may look like fish as they dive and swim gracefully through the seas, but they are in fact small whales. Like all **whales**, dolphins are **mammals**, not fish.

Dolphins have smooth, sleek skin and a torpedo-shaped body to help them swim easily through water. Most dolphins have a tail **fin** and a large curved fin in the middle of their back. They also have two **flippers**, one on each side of the body. Dolphins have a long **snout**, which is sometimes called a beak. Inside this snout there may be up to 200 small teeth. Dolphins can be black, white, grey, yellow, brown, pink or a mix of colours. Some are spotted or even striped!

This is a bottlenose dolphin. Dolphins are mammals and breathe air as we do. Dolphin mothers give birth to live young and feed their babies milk from their bodies.

Heinemann InfoSearch

Life in a School

Dolphins

Heinemann
LIBRARY

Richard and Louise Spilsbury

www.heinemann.co.uk/library

To order:
☎ Phone 44 (0) 1865 888066
▤ Send a fax to 44 (0) 1865 314091
▭ Visit the Heinemann Bookshop at www.heinemann.co.uk/library to browse our catalogue and order online.

First published in Great Britain by Heinemann Library, Halley Court, Jordan Hill, Oxford OX2 8EJ, part of Harcourt Education.
Heinemann is a registered trademark of Harcourt Education Ltd.

Editorial: Nicole Irving and Georga Godwin
Design: Ron Kamen and Celia Floyd
Picture Research: Rebecca Sodergren and Ginny Stroud-Lewis
Production: Viv Hichens

Originated by Dot Gradations Ltd
Printed in China by WKT Company Limited

ISBN 0 431 18264 7 (hardback)
08 07 06 05 04
10 9 8 7 6 5 4 3 2 1

ISBN 0 431 18271 X (paperback)
09 08 07 06 05
10 9 8 7 6 5 4 3 2 1

British Library Cataloguing in Publication Data

Spilsbury, Richard and Spilsbury, Louise
Animal Groups: Dolphins – Life in a School
599.5'3156
A full catalogue record for this book is available from the British Library.

Acknowledgements

The Publishers would like to thank the following for permission to reproduce photographs:

Corbis p. 19; Corbis/George D. Lepp p. 8; FLPA/Foto Naturastock p. 15; FLPA/marinelane p. 20; FLPA/Minden Pictures/Flip Nicklin p. 23; FLPA/Nicklin/Minden p. 25; Image Bank p. 21; NHPA/Norbert Wu p. 14; NPL/Doc White p. 18; NPL/Jeff Rotman p. 12; NPL/Martha Holes p. 28; NPL/Tom Walmsley pp. 4, 10; NPL/Sue Flood p. 26; Oxford Scientific Films/David Fleetham p. 6; Oxford Scientific Films/Des and Jen Bartlett p. 24; Oxford Scientific Films/Doug Allen p. 17; Oxfrod Scientific Films/Gerard Soury pp. 11, 22; Oxford Scientific Films/Howard Hall p. 23; Oxford Scientific Films/Konrad Wothe p. 9; Oxford Scientific Films/Will Darnell/Animals Animals p. 27; Still Pictures/Roland Seitre p. 16.

Cover photograph of the school of dolphins, reproduced with permission of FLPA/Minden Pictures/Flip Nicklin.

The Publishers would like to thank Colin Fountain for his assistance in the preparation of this book.

Every effort has been made to contact copyright holders of any material reproduced in this book. Any omissions will be rectified in subsequent printings if notice is given to the Publishers.

Kinds of dolphins

There are about 32 different **species** (kinds) of dolphins across the world. There are also six different species of porpoises, which are very similar to dolphins. Porpoises live in very similar ways to dolphins but they are smaller and faster and have different shaped teeth.

Living in groups

Dolphins are among the most intelligent animals in the world. Each individual dolphin has its own personality, just like people. Some dolphins are shy; others are show-offs. Some dolphins are very bright; others are a little slower to learn. They may do some things on their own but dolphins are **social** animals and spend most of their lives in groups. A group of dolphins is usually called a school or pod.

This is a group of Common dolphins. When you see dolphins travelling, they are usually together in schools like this, or with a few members from the same group.

What is a dolphin school like?

Schools of dolphins vary greatly in size. Bottlenose dolphin schools can be as small as a couple of individuals or as many as 500. Most common dolphin schools have between 20 and 500 individuals, but the largest can have tens of thousands of members out in the open ocean. River dolphins usually form small family groups of about five dolphins.

Groups within a school

Many large schools of dolphins contain **males** and **females**, and dolphins of all ages. Some dolphins form schools in other ways. Nursery groups contain mothers, their daughters and all their **calves**. The adult males form separate **bachelor pods**. Some kinds of dolphins form groups according to age. For example, young adult dusky dolphins form separate schools to the older adults.

Dolphins may spend some time in small groups with five or six other dolphins from their school. Later, these small groups join together to feed or travel.

Why do dolphins live in a school?

Dolphins live in groups to help each other. Dolphins in a school help each other catch food, spot danger and care for calves. Dolphins take care of sick or injured dolphins in their school and also seem to enjoy each other's company!

Dolphins need to swim to the surface regularly to breathe. If a dolphin is too tired, injured or sick to do this it may die. In a school of dolphins, there is usually someone on hand to give you a nudge up!

Who's who in a school?

In most schools of dolphins, some animals are more **dominant** than others. The larger or stronger male dolphins are usually dominant. Dominant males have a better chance of **mating** with female dolphins. They also get to swim at the top of the school, where it is easy for them to go to the surface to breathe.

Where do dolphins live?

There are dolphins in all oceans of the world, from the cold waters near the North and South **Poles**, to warm **tropical** waters. Some kinds of dolphins live only in one part of the world. The New Zealand dolphin, as its name suggests, is only found in waters around New Zealand. Other dolphins, such as the bottlenose, are found in most of the world's oceans.

Some **species** of dolphins live in waters close to land. The five species of river dolphins live only in particular rivers and **estuaries**. Other kinds of dolphins spend all their lives far out at sea. Many dolphins live in different places at different times of the year. In summer, southern right whale dolphins live in waters around Antarctica. In winter, they move further north, following the **shoals** of fish they like to eat.

This Pacific white-sided dolphin lives in the cold sea around British Columbia, Canada.

How do dolphins keep warm?

Mammals that live on land usually have hair on their bodies for warmth. **Whales** and dolphins have little or no hair, so how do they keep warm when swimming in cold or deep water? Dolphins have a thick layer of blubber (fat) under their skin to keep them warm. The blubber stops them losing their body warmth to the cold around them.

How far do they travel?

Many dolphins live, swim and feed in one particular area for most of the time. This is called their home range. Dolphin schools have ranges of different sizes. For example, spotted dolphins have a roughly circular home range, which is around 250 miles (400 kilometres) in diameter within which they travel around 45 miles (70 kilometres) a day. They search for food, rest, live and have young here.

These bottlenose dolphins are swimming in the warm tropical waters of the Caribbean.

How do dolphins swim?

A dolphin's body is perfectly **adapted** to its life in the water. Its **streamlined** shape helps the dolphin move smoothly through water. The bones that make up a dolphin's skeleton are filled with fat and **oil**. This makes them a lot lighter than bones like ours, and helps to keep the dolphin from sinking. A dolphin uses the powerful **muscles** along its back to move its tail **flukes** up and down. This moves it forward through the water.

How fast can dolphins swim?

Most dolphins swim at about 6 to 9 miles (10 to 15 kilometres) per hour most of the time, while people usually walk at about 2 miles (about 3 kilometres) per hour. Dolphins can speed up to just over 30 miles (50 kilometres) an hour if they need to make a quick getaway.

This Common dolphin is bow riding. Many dolphins do this. They use the force of water pushed in front of a moving boat to help them move along.

When a dolphin swims, it uses its **flippers** to steer, turn, slow down and, with the help of the flukes, to stop. Many dolphins also have a dorsal (back) **fin**. This helps to keep a dolphin straight up in the water as it swims.

How long can dolphins stay underwater?

Most dolphins can stay underwater for about ten minutes at a time. Then they have to come back up to the surface to breathe. Dolphins breathe through their **blowhole**. When they swim underwater they have to hold their breath. As they dive, a **muscular** skin flap covers the blowhole. This stops water entering the blowhole and getting into their **lungs**, which would drown them.

When dolphins are swimming along quickly, some types, such as these Atlantic spotted dolphins leap right out of the water to take a quick breath of air before swimming on.

What do dolphins eat?

All dolphins are **carnivores** – they eat other animals. Most kinds of dolphins eat fish and squid, although dolphins eat different kinds of foods, depending on where they live. As well as fish, river dolphins eat crab and clams from the river bed. Some dolphins eat a variety of foods, others eat only one kind – Risso's dolphins eat mainly squid, for example. Some dolphins, such as the Pacific white-sided dolphin, usually eat fish that live in large **shoals**, such as anchovies and mackerel.

Bottlenose dolphins have about twenty pairs of small, cone-shaped teeth that they use to catch jellyfish, squid and a wide variety of fish and shellfish.

How do dolphins eat?

A dolphin grabs and tears its **prey** with its many sharp teeth. All dolphins swallow their food whole or in large chunks because they do not have flat-topped teeth for chewing. Each day, dolphins eat up to one-third of their own body weight in food!

How do dolphins find food?

Most dolphins can see quite well, but it can be hard to see very far in rivers, seas and oceans. It gets dark deep underwater and shallow waters may be murky. Sound travels well in water, and dolphins have very good hearing, so they use sound rather than sight to find their **prey**.

What is echolocation?

Dolphins use **echolocation** to locate prey and to find their way around in dark waters. They send out a series of clicks and other sounds that echo (bounce back) from fish or other objects that the sounds hit in the water. By listening to the echoes reflected back to it, a dolphin can tell what shape an object is and therefore what it is. The dolphin can also tell how far away it is and in which direction.

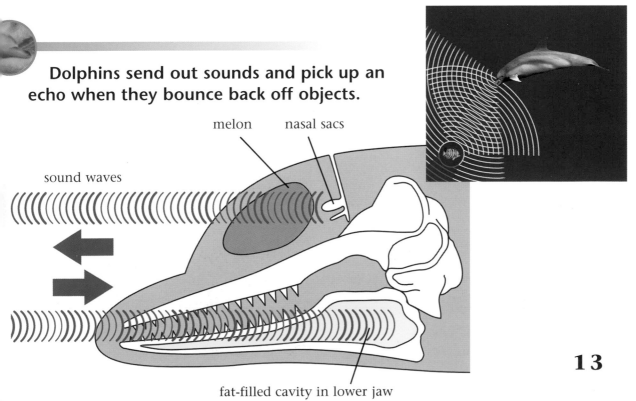

Dolphins send out sounds and pick up an echo when they bounce back off objects.

melon   nasal sacs

sound waves

fat-filled cavity in lower jaw

13

How do dolphins make echolocation sounds?

When dolphins make echolocation sounds they do not open their mouths. They make the sounds inside their heads – a bit like when you hum. When the clicks echo back to the dolphin they travel through its lower **jaw** and into its inner ear. The brain then works out what the sounds mean.

Most dolphins have quite large brows, although some are more obvious than others. A dolphin's rounded brow is called a melon, because it looks a similar shape to a melon fruit. In fact, a dolphin's melon is a swollen part filled with fluid. It changes shape very slightly to focus (aim) the clicks a dolphin sends out to use for echolocation. A dolphin's melon can help it to recognize even tiny prey a few millimetres across!

Echolocation is important for river dolphins, because most live in murky waters. They, and some other dolphins, move their head from side to side as they swim to spread their echolocation clicks all around.

How do dolphin schools hunt?

Individual dolphins sometimes feed by themselves, but most often they hunt together in teams. Dolphins are very intelligent, and dolphin schools use a variety of hunting methods. Different kinds of dolphins may use different hunting tactics. Methods also vary depending on what **prey** the dolphin school is trying to catch. Sometimes schools of different kinds of dolphins work together because many eat the same kinds of fish.

This Risso's dolphin is 'spy-hopping'. Dolphins sometimes raise their heads well out of the water to scan around for prey.

Hunting tactics

Groups of dolphins that live in the open ocean may hunt by swimming in circles around a **shoal** of fish. Gradually the circles they swim in become smaller and smaller, forcing the fish to form a tight shoal in the middle. Then the dolphins can swim through the tightly packed fish and eat.

Working together

Dolphins in a school take it in turns to feed. Some remain at the edge making sure the shoal does not break up and the fish escape, while others eat. Dolphins that hunt closer to shore often work together to chase fish into shallow water. Some dolphins keep the fish trapped in the shallows, while others feed.

Do dolphins ever team up with people? ● ● ● ● ● ● ● ● ● ●

In some parts of the world, dolphin schools work with humans as a way of getting food. Atlantic humpback dolphins have learnt that if they chase large shoals of fish towards fishing nets near the shore, the fishermen will throw them a share of the catch as a reward.

Large schools of Common dolphins may work together to chase fish and force them to the surface of the water where it is impossible for them to escape.

These bottlenose dolphins have chased fish onto a muddy shore in the USA. They have to be careful that they do not end up too far up the beach, as they may not be able to get back to sea.

How do dolphins care for their young?

Most dolphins can have young at any time of the year. Different kinds of dolphins may carry babies for different lengths of time, but most baby dolphins are born nine to twelve months after parents have **mated**. Most adult **female** dolphins have a baby every two years.

Most dolphin babies are born just below the surface of the water. They are usually born tail first and can swim within minutes of being born. In many schools, other dolphins help the mother with the birth. Bottlenose dolphins may tug gently at the baby's tail as it comes out. They also protect the baby from any sharks that come by, attracted by the smell of the blood released during the birth.

Some kinds of dolphins, like these Atlantic spotted dolphins, even swim together as a group to help a young dolphin up to the surface to take a breath!

What are dolphin babies like?

Dolphin babies are called **calves**. Most calves look like little versions of their parents. Some kinds of dolphins look different when they are young to how they will look as adults. For example, they may be a slightly different colour or they may not develop adult patterning until they are older. Most dolphin babies are about 1 metre long when they are born, but this is different for some smaller **species**.

What do dolphin babies feed on?

Calves **suckle** milk from their mother underwater. Dolphin milk, like most **mammal** milk, is very rich in fat. It is a complete food for babies in the first part of their life, and it even provides the water they need. Calves only suckle for a few minutes at a time because they have to go to the surface regularly to breathe.

Spotted dolphin calves like the one in this picture are born grey all over. They only get their spots when they are older.

When do calves stop suckling?

Dolphin calves suckle for about a year to eighteen months. From about six months old, most calves begin to eat some fish as well as suckle their mother's milk. Calves remain close to their mother's side for the first few years of life, even when they no longer need to suckle. Fathers usually return to **bachelor pods**, so they do not really help look after the calves. Other dolphins in the mother's school help to care for them.

How do young dolphins learn?

It is important for young dolphins to spend time with other members of their school. This close contact helps them to get to know the other dolphins and to learn how to behave. Young dolphins also learn how to swim, catch fish, **communicate** and join in a hunt by watching and copying adults in their school.

A dolphin calf suckles from two nipples on its mother's belly. The mother's rich milk helps a baby grow quickly.

How does a dolphin school help to raise calves?

When a mother needs to rest or wants to go off to feed without her calf, she usually leaves it with some young female dolphins from her school. This helps the mother, but it also teaches the young females. The babysitters learn how to care for calves so they will be better mothers when they grow up.

When is a dolphin grown up?

Dolphins, like many other animals, are counted as adults when they are old enough to have young of their own. Different species of dolphins become adults at different ages. A bottlenose dolphin is an adult when it is around eight to ten years old.

When young Atlantic spotted dolphins swim with their mothers and other dolphins, they learn about life in a school.

Dolphins spend a large portion of every day playing. Dolphins have very sensitive skin and they touch and nudge each other a lot when they chase and swim together. Dolphins often play with 'toys', such as seaweed or feathers, which they throw to each other or toss around. They may even surf in waves breaking near the shore. As well as being fun, play improves **echolocation** and swimming skills, and helps to keep the dolphins feeling like a group.

How do dolphins sleep?

Unlike humans, dolphins have to think about their breathing when they sleep. Each side of a dolphin's brain takes it in turn to rest, while the other stays alert to make sure the dolphin breathes. Some dolphins lie horizontally on the water's surface so their **blowhole** is always open to the air.

This bottlenose dolphin is taking a short nap for a few moments while it is swimming along.

Spinner dolphins can spin their body as many as seven times in a single leap. Many scientists believe they leap and spin together just for fun!

Sailors and divers have often seen dolphins playing with objects – these spotted dolphins are tossing and chasing a red scarf!

23

How do dolphins communicate?

When they hunt in teams, dolphins have to **communicate** to keep in touch with each other. They also communicate to warn each other of danger and to tell others food is nearby. Dolphins usually communicate using sound. Dolphins make lots of different sounds, including rattles, clicks, rasps and whistles. They may make a kind of barking sound when they are angry or squeak when they are being playful.

When a dolphin leaps high in the air like this we call it breaching. **Males** often breach to attract the attention of a **female**.

Body language

Body language is when you use a part of your body to communicate, as we do when we scowl, point or wave. When dolphins are close enough to see each other, they also use body language. The most noticeable bit of dolphin body language is 'breaching'. This is when one dolphin leaps out of the water to make other dolphins notice it.

Male bottlenose dolphins twist their body into an S shape to tell the females they are ready to **mate**. Dolphins often show togetherness by swimming closely, side by side. The direction at which one dolphin swims towards another also has a special meaning. If a dolphins approaches quickly from the front or side it may mean it is angry.

Dolphins often rub pectoral (back) **fins**, like this, when they meet. This is a sort of greeting, similar to a handshake or hug between two people.

Whistle names

In many **species**, each dolphin in a school has its own personal whistle sound, rather like having its own name. One dolphin may imitate (mimic) another dolphin's whistle to get its attention, just as you call out a friend's name. Sometimes many dolphins in a school whistle at once, repeating their whistle names again and again. This helps them keep in touch with each other.

Do dolphins fight?

Male dolphins fight over **female** dolphins when they are ready to **mate**. They may also fight over food. Before fighting, a dolphin tries to warn off another by using **displays**. These are meant to show that it would win a fight if it comes to it. A male warning display might involve darting about, slapping its tail on the water's surface and blowing water out of its **blowhole**. Another signal that they are ready to fight is a sharp, sideways head jerk with closed or open **jaws**.

If these displays do not scare off the other dolphin, the two fight. Dolphins fight by ramming or butting each other with their hard noses, striking with their tail or biting. They use their teeth to make scratches, called rake marks, on each other's skin.

This Risso's dolphin was probably scarred by other Risso's dolphins using their front teeth when fighting.

Orcas (killer **whales**) and some kinds of shark are the only wild **predators** that hunt and eat dolphins. Even if dolphins are not killed when a shark or orca tries to catch them, they may die later from the wounds these predators can make.

The main reason dolphins have so few predators is that if a dolphin is attacked the school works together to protect it. For example, if a shark moves in on a dolphin, the other dolphins in its school form a circle and work together to ram the shark to chase it off. Even great white sharks and orcas are far less likely to attack dolphins when they are in large schools.

The maximum length of an adult orca, or killer whale, is about 10 metres. It has a powerful body that makes it an effective predator. Like dolphins, orcas are **social** animals that often hunt in teams.

27

Do people harm dolphins?

People are a dolphin's biggest danger. Many fishing boats use huge nets that trap other animals, along with the sharks and fish they are meant to catch. Many dolphins drown when they are caught in fishing nets because they cannot get to the surface to breathe. Lots of people prefer to buy tuna with a 'Dolphin Friendly' label, which means the fish was caught on long lines and hooks that do not harm dolphins.

In some parts of the world, people hunt dolphins for food. **Pollution** in the oceans, such as old fishing nets and other rubbish, as well as fuel **oil** leaked or dumped from ships also causes serious problems for sea animals like dolphins.

In some places fishermen with vast nets are taking so many fish from the sea that there are not enough left for dolphins and other sea animals to eat. This is called 'overfishing'.